Especially for

Marilee

From

Barb

Date

12/20/12

Written and compiled by Ellyn Sanna.

ISBN 978-1-61626-320-1

Published by Barbour Publishing, Inc., P.O. Box 719, Uhrichsville, Ohio 44683, www.barbourbooks.com

Our mission is to publish and distribute inspirational products offering exceptional value and biblical encouragement to the masses.

Member of the
Evangelical Christian
Publishers Association

Printed in China.

power
of
simple living

BARBOUR
PUBLISHING

Introduction

Our world is so complicated. Despite today's time-saving conveniences, everyone seems to get busier and busier. Now and then, it's good to take a step back and take a fresh look at our lives—and realize that

the simple things are what matter most in life. As we focus on those things—the everyday joys of sunshine and laughter, friendship and quiet times, and most of all God's grace—we find rest for our hearts and new strength for our days. There is truly power in living more simply!

There is no shortage of good days.
It is good lives that are hard to come by.
A life of good days lived in the senses is not
enough. The life of sensation is the life of greed;
it requires more and more. The life of the
spirit requires less and less; time is ample
and its passage sweet.
ANNIE DILLARD

• • • • •

When a man's knowledge is not in order,
the more of it he has, the greater will
be his confusion of thought.
HERBERT SPENCER

I went to the woods because I wished
to live deliberately, to front only the essential
facts of life, and see if I could not learn what
it had to teach, and not, when I came to die,
discover that I had not lived.

HENRY DAVID THOREAU

• • • • •

Better to have little, with godliness,
than to be rich and dishonest.

PROVERBS 16:8 NLT

A man is rich in proportion to the number
of things he can afford to let alone.
HENRY DAVID THOREAU

• • • • •

Measure your wealth in smiles,
in friendships, and in love-filled moments.
What good is a bank account without
these simple and everyday coins?
LORNA PRESTON

• • • • •

Simplicity is the ultimate sophistication.
LEONARDO DA VINCI

I have three precious things that
I hold fast and prize. The first is gentleness;
the second is frugality; the third is humility,
which keeps me from putting myself before
others. Be gentle and you can be bold;
be frugal and you can be generous.

LAO TZU

• • • • • •

He will always be a slave who does
not know how to live upon a little.

HORACE

Waste neither time nor money, but make the best use of both. Without industry and frugality, nothing will do, and with them everything.

BENJAMIN FRANKLIN

• • • • • • •

Set aside a certain number of days,
during which you shall be content with
the scantiest and cheapest fare, with course
and rough dress, saying to yourself the while:
"Is this the condition that I feared?"

SENECA

Cultivate these, then, for they
are wholly within your power:
sincerity and dignity, industriousness,
and sobriety. Avoid grumbling.
Be frugal, considerate, and honest;
be temperate in manner and speech.

MARCUS AURELIUS

You can't force simplicity;
but you can invite it in by finding as much
richness as possible in the few things at hand.
Simplicity doesn't mean meagerness but rather a
certain kind of richness, the fullness that appears
when we stop stuffing the world with things.
THOMAS MOORE

• • • • •

My riches consist not in the extent of my
possessions but in the fewness of my wants.
J. BOTHERTON

We substitute the joy of ownership for the desire
of accumulation. Luxuries become necessities.
The tyranny of things overwhelms the
acquisitive heart.
FRED SMITH

• • • • •

Happiness is a flower that thrives
in simplicity. Too many possessions
are like weeds that crowd it out.
AILENE BASCOMBE

A devout life does bring wealth. . .
the rich simplicity of being yourself before God.
1 Timothy 6:6 msg

• • • • •

And to make it your ambition to lead
a quiet life and attend to your own
business and work with your hands.
1 Thessalonians 4:11 nasb

To find the universal elements
enough; to find the air and the water
exhilarating; to be refreshed by a
morning walk or an evening saunter. . .
to be thrilled by the stars at night;
to be elated over a bird's nest or a
wildflower in spring—these are some
of the rewards of the simple life.

JOHN BURROUGHS

The foolish man seeks happiness in the distance;
the wise grows it under his feet.
JAMES OPENHEIM

• • • • •

Reduce the complexity of life by
eliminating the needless wants of life,
and the labors of life reduce themselves.
EDWIN TEALE

Often people attempt to live their lives backwards; they try to have more things or more money in order to do more of what they want, so they will be happier. The way it actually works is the reverse. You must first be who you really are, then do what you need to do, in order to have what you want.

MARGARET YOUNG

We tend to forget that happiness doesn't come as a result of getting something we don't have, but rather of recognizing and appreciating what we do have.

FREDERICK KEONIG

● ● ● ● ●

Grace isn't a little prayer you chant before receiving a meal. It's a way to live.

JACQUELINE WINSPEAR

If you want to turn your life around,
try thankfulness. It will change
your life mightily.
GERALD GOOD

• • • • •

Not everything that can be
counted counts, and not everything
that counts can be counted.
ALBERT EINSTEIN

The point in life is to know what's enough.
GENSEI

• • • • •

The glow of one warm thought is
worth more to me than money.
THOMAS JEFFERSON

• • • • •

To know you have enough is to be rich.
LAO TZU

Voluntary simplicity means going
fewer places in one day rather than more,
seeing less so I can see more, doing less so I can
do more, acquiring less so I can have more.

JOHN KABAT-ZINN

● ● ● ● ● ● ●

Gratitude unlocks the fullness of life.
It turns what we have into enough, and more. . . .
It can turn a meal into a feast, a house into a home,
a stranger into a friend. Gratitude makes
sense of our past, brings peace for today,
and creates a vision for tomorrow.

MELODY BEATTIE

Best of all is it to preserve everything in a pure,
still heart, and let there be for every pulse
a thanksgiving, and for every breath a song.
KONRAD VON GESNER

. . . . .

Dear Lord, we beg but one boon more:
Peace in the hearts of all men living,
peace in the whole world this Thanksgiving.
JOSEPH AUSLANDER

When I chased after money, I never had
enough. When I got my life on purpose and
focused on giving of myself and everything that
arrived into my life, then I was prosperous.
WAYNE DYER

• • • • •

The things that are essential are acquired
with little bother; it is the luxuries that call
for toil and effort. To want simply what is
enough nowadays suggests to people
primitiveness and squalor.
SENECA

Discover that you have enough, let go of trying to
get more of what you don't really need,
and refocus the energy that's been devoted to
acquiring more toward what you already have.
LYNNE TWIST

• • • • • • • •

The day, water, sun, moon, night—
I do not have to purchase these
things with money.
PLAUTUS

For he will be like a tree planted by the water,
that extends its roots by a stream and will not fear
when the heat comes; but its leaves will be green,
and it will not be anxious in a year of drought
nor cease to yield fruit.

JEREMIAH 17:8 NASB

• • • • • • • •

"So don't worry about these things, saying,
'What will we eat? What will we drink?
What will we wear?' These things dominate the
thoughts of unbelievers, but your heavenly
Father already knows all your needs."

MATTHEW 6:31–32 NLT

The real measure of your wealth is how much
you'd be worth if you lost all your money.
UNKNOWN

· · · · · · ·

Money is not required to buy
one necessity of the soul.
HENRY DAVID THOREAU

· · · · · · ·

We make ourselves rich by
making our wants few.
HENRY DAVID THOREAU

Less is more.
Mies van der Rohe

Frugality is one of the most
beautiful and joyful words in the
English language, and yet one that
we are culturally cut off from
understanding and enjoying.
The consumption society has made
us feel that happiness lies in having
things, and has failed to teach us the
happiness of not having things.
ELISE BOULDING

To poke a wood fire is more solid enjoyment
than almost anything else in the world.
CHARLES DUDLEY WARNER

•   •   •   •   •

Eliminate physical clutter. More importantly,
eliminate spiritual clutter.
TERRI GUILLEMETS

•   •   •   •   •

Everything should be made as simple as
possible, but not simpler.
ALBERT EINSTEIN

The ability to simplify means to eliminate the unnecessary so that the necessary may speak.
HANS HOFMANN

• • • • •

Any intelligent fool can make things bigger, more complex, and more violent. It takes a touch of genius—and a lot of courage— to move in the opposite direction.
E. F. SCHUMACHER

Life is really simple,
but we insist on making it complicated.
CONFUCIUS

• • • • •

Simplicity is making the journey of
this life with just baggage enough.
UNKNOWN

• • • • •

The trouble with simple living is that,
though it can be joyful, rich, and creative,
it isn't simple.
DORIS JANZEN LONGACRE

Everything we possess that is not necessary
for life or happiness becomes a burden,
and scarcely a day passes that we do not add to it.
ROBERT BRAULT

• • • • • • •

I like to walk about among the beautiful things
that adorn the world; but private wealth I should
decline, or any sort of personal possessions,
because they would take away my liberty.
GEORGE SANTAYANA

The best things in life are nearest:
Breath in your nostrils, light in your eyes,
flowers at your feet, duties at your hand,
the path of right just before you. Then do not grasp
at the stars, but do life's plain,
common work as it comes, certain that daily duties
and daily bread are the sweetest things in life.
ROBERT LOUIS STEVENSON

• • • • • • • •

Material blessings,
when they pay beyond the category of need,
are weirdly fruitful of headache.
PHILIP WYLIE

Live simply that others might simply live.
ELIZABETH SEATON

• • • • • • • •

Besides the noble art of getting things done,
there is the noble art of leaving things undone.
The wisdom of life consists in the elimination
of non-essentials.
LIN YUTANG

By wisdom a house is built,
and by understanding it is established;
and by knowledge the rooms are filled
with all precious and pleasant riches.
PROVERBS 24:3–4 NASB

* * * * *

Seek the Kingdom of God above all else,
and live righteously, and he will give
you everything you need.
MATTHEW 6:33 NLT

As you simplify your life,
the laws of the universe will be simpler;
solitude will not be solitude, poverty will
not be poverty, nor weakness weakness.
HENRY DAVID THOREAU

• • • • •

Have nothing in your houses that you do not
know to be useful or believe to be beautiful.
WILLIAM MORRIS

Anything simple always interests me.
DAVID HOCKNEY

• • • •

Our affluent society contains those of
talent and insight who are driven to prefer
poverty, to choose it, rather than submit to
the desolation of an empty abundance.
MICHAEL HARRINGTON

How many things are there
which I do not want.

SOCRATES

More good has been accomplished by simple
people seeking their own honest ends than
by all the philanthropists in history.
ROBERT BRAULT

• • • • •

Remember that in giving any reason
at all for refusing, you lay some
foundation for a future request.
ARTHUR HELPS

[He] sets no price upon either his property or his labor. His generosity is limited only by his strength and ability. He regards it as an honor to be selected for difficult or dangerous service and would think it shameful to ask for any reward.

OHIYESA OF THE SANTEE SIOUX

You have succeeded in life
when all you really want is
only what you really need.

VERNON HOWARD

Simplicity, simplicity, simplicity!
I say, let your affairs be as two or three,
and not a hundred or a thousand instead
of a million count half a dozen,
and keep your accounts on your thumbnail.
HENRY DAVID THOREAU

• • • • •

The greatest truths are the simplest:
so likewise are the greatest men.
AUGUSTUS WILLIAM HARE
JULIUS CHARLES HARE

Be content with what you have,
rejoice in the way things are.
When you realize there is nothing lacking,
the whole world belongs to you.
LAO TZU

• • • • • • •

We don't need to increase our goods nearly as
much as we need to scale down our wants.
Not wanting something is as good
as possessing it.
DONALD HORBAN

For I have learned to be content in whatever circumstances I am. I know how to get along with humble means, and I also know how to live in prosperity; in any and every circumstance I have learned the secret of being filled and going hungry, both of having abundance and suffering need. I can do all things through Him who strengthens me.

PHILIPPIANS 4:11–13 NASB

The sculptor produces the beautiful statue by chipping away such parts of the marble block as are not needed—it is a process of elimination.

ELBERT HUBBARD

• • • • •

It is the sweet, simple things of life which are the real ones after all.

LAURA INGALLS WILDER

"Think simple" as my old master used to say.
Reduce the whole of its parts into the simplest terms,
getting back to first principles.
FRANK LLOYD WRIGHT

• • • • • • •

Things turn out best for the people who make
the best out of the way things turn out.
ART LINKLETTER

To live content with small means;
to seek elegance rather than luxury,
and refinement rather than fashion; to be worthy,
not respectable, and wealthy, not rich;
to listen to stars and birds, babes and sages,
with open heart; to study hard; to think quietly,
act frankly, talk gently, await occasions, hurry never;
in a word, to let the spiritual, unbidden and
unconscious, grow up through the common—
this is my symphony.

WILLIAM HENRY CHANNING

Only those who have the patience to do
simple things perfectly will acquire the skill
to do difficult things easily.
JOHANN SCHILLER

• • • • •

No person can be lost by following
the simple and well-beaten path of
ordinary devotion and prayer.
R. H. BENSON

Great things are done by a series of
small things brought together.
VINCENT VAN GOGH

• • •

Train yourself to listen to that
small voice that tells us what's
important and what's not.
SUE GRAFTON

• • •

We can do no great things,
only small things with great love.
MOTHER TERESA

Two things are written in stone:
1. Kindness in another's troubles.
2. Courage in your own.
ADAM LINDSAY GORDON

• • • • •

Whatever you're working on, take small bites.
The task will not be overwhelming if you
can reduce it to its smallest component.
RICHARD RUSSO

When you can do the common things
of life in an uncommon way,
you will command the attention of the world.
GEORGE WASHINGTON CARVER

• • • • •

Cheerfulness, it would appear, is a matter
which depends fully as much on the state of
things within, as on the state of things
without and around us.
CHARLOTTE BRONTË

If the sight of the blue skies fills you with joy,
if a blade of grass springing up in the fields
has power to move you, if the simple things of
nature have a message that you understand,
rejoice, for your soul is alive.

ELEONORA DUSE

The next time it begins to rain. . .
lie down on your belly, nestle your
chin into the grass, and get a frog's—
eye view of how raindrops fall. . . .
The sight of hundreds of blades of
grass bowing down and popping back
up like piano keys strikes me as one of
the merriest sights in the world.

MALCOLM MARGOLIN

All the great things are simple, and many
can be expressed in a single word:
freedom; justice; honor; duty; mercy; hope.
Sir Winston Churchill

• • • • •

Be faithful in small things because it
is in them that your strength lies.
Mother Teresa

*Since we entered the world penniless
and will leave it penniless,
if we have bread on the table and
shoes on our feet, that's enough.*
1 TIMOTHY 6:7–8 MSG

• • • •

*The LORD is my shepherd;
I have all that I need.*
PSALM 23:1 NLT

Nothing is worth more than this day.
JOHANN WOLFGANG VON GOETHE

· · · · ·

What we put into every moment is all we have.
GILDA RADNER

· · · · ·

Seize the day, and put the least
possible trust in tomorrow.
HORACE

Eternity is not something that begins after you are dead. It is going on all the time. We are in it now.

CHARLOTTE PERKINS GILMAN

• • • • • • • •

I choose to inhabit my days, to allow my living to open me, to make me less afraid, more accessible, to loosen my heart until it becomes a wing, a torch, a promise.

DAWNA MARKOVA

Friends, books, a garden,
and perhaps his pen,
Delightful industry enjoy'd at home,
And Nature, in her cultivated trim
Dress'ed to his taste,
inviting him abroad—
Can he want occupation
who has these?

WILLIAM COWPER

I am convinced both by faith and experience,
that to maintain one's self on this earth
is not a hardship but a pastime,
if we will live simply and wisely.
HENRY DAVID THOREAU

● ● ● ● ● ● ●

If I had my life to live over. . .
I would perhaps have more actual troubles,
but I'd have fewer imaginary ones.
NADINE STAIR

Be wary of any enterprise
that requires new clothes.
HENRY DAVID THOREAU

• • • • • • • •

The little things? The little moments?
They aren't little.
JOHN ZABAT-ZINN

• • • • • • • •

I'm living so far beyond my income that we
may almost be said to be living apart.
E. E. CUMMINGS

With a few flowers in my garden,
half a dozen pictures and some books,
I live without envy.
LOPE DE VEGA

• • • • •

Making the simple complicated is commonplace;
making the complicated simple,
awesomely simple, that's creativity.
CHARLES MINGUS

Abandon the urge to simplify everything,
to look for formulas and easy answers,
and to begin to think multidimensionally,
to glory in the mystery and paradoxes of
life, not to be dismayed by the multitude
of causes and consequences that are
inherent in each experience—
to appreciate the fact that life is complex.
M. SCOTT PECK

Manifest plainness,
Embrace simplicity,
Reduce selfishness,
Have few desires.
LAO TZU

•　•　•　•　•

Most of the critical things in life,
which become the starting points
for human destiny, are little things.
R. SMITH

When speech comes from a quiet heart,
it has the strength of the orchid
and the fragrance of rock.
STEPHEN MITCHELL

• • • • •

Enjoy the little things, for one day you may look
back and realize they were the big things.
ROBERT BRAULT

*And God is able to make all grace abound to you,
so that always having all sufficiency in everything,
you may have an abundance for every good deed.*
2 CORINTHIANS 9:8 NASB

• • • • • • •

*And my God will supply all your needs according
to His riches in glory in Christ Jesus.*
PHILIPPIANS 4:19 NASB

The more we strive to fit into our schedules,
the more hungry our hearts become.
Simplicity feeds the heart.
ABNER BUTTONWOOD

• • • • •

Life engenders life. Energy creates energy.
It is by spending oneself that one becomes rich.
SARAH BERNHARDT

The art of contentment is the recognition
that the most satisfying and the most
dependably refreshing experiences of life
lie not in great things but in little.
The rarity of happiness among those
who achieved much is evidence that
achievement is not in itself the assurance
of a happy life. The great, like the humble,
may have to find their satisfaction
in the same plain things.

EDGAR A. COLLARD

Stars over snow, and in the west a planet
swinging below a star—look for a lovely
thing and you will find it, it is not far—
it never will be far.
Sara Teasdale

·　·　·　·　·

What worth has beauty, if it is not seen?
Italian Proverb

Too many people spend
money they haven't earned,
to buy things they don't want,
to impress people they don't like.
WILL ROGERS

When I dance, I dance, when I sleep, I sleep; yes, and when I walk alone in a beautiful orchard, if my thoughts drift to far-off matters for some part of the time, for some other part I lead them back again to the walk, the orchard, to the sweetness of this solitude, to myself.

MONTAIGNE

Desired substance, things, patterns, or sequences of experience that are in some sense "good" for the organism—items of diet, conditions of life, temperature, entertainment, sex, and so forth— are never such that more of the something is always better than less of the something. Rather, for all objects and experiences, there is a quantity that has optimum value. Above that quantity, the variable becomes toxic. To fall below that value is to be deprived.

GREGORY BATESON

The aspects of things that are most important to us are hidden because of their simplicity and familiarity.

LUDWIG WITTGENSTEIN

• • • • •

Precisely the least, the softest, lightest, a lizard's rustling, a breath, a flash, a moment—a little makes the way of the best happiness.

FREDERICH NIETZSCHE

I never had any other desire so strong,
and so like covetousness, as that. . . .
I might be master at last of a small
house and a large garden,
with very moderate conveniences
joined to them, and there dedicate the
remainder of my life to the culture of
them and the study of nature.

ABRAHAM COWLEY

We struggle with the complexities
and avoid the simplicities.
NORMAN VINCENT PEALE

• • • • •

The simplest things give me ideas.
JOAN MIRO

There is no time to waste,
so don't complicate your lives
unnecessarily. Keep it simple—
in marriage, grief, joy, whatever.
Even in ordinary things—your daily
routines of shopping and so on.
Deal as sparingly as possible with the
things the world thrusts on you.
This world as you see it is on its way out.
1 CORINTHIANS 7:28–30 MSG

The point in life is to know what's enough—
why envy those otherworld immortals?
With the happiness held in one inch-square
heart you can fill the whole space
between heaven and earth.

GENSEI

• • • • • •

The point of philosophy is to start with
something so simple as not to seem worth
stating, and to end with something so
paradoxical that no one will believe it.

BERTRAND RUSSELL

If you have a garden and a library,
you have everything you need.
CICERO

• • • • •

Nature uses as little as possible of anything.
JOHANNES KEPPLER

• • • • •

Simplicity is the essence of happiness.
CEDRIC BLEDSOE

While washing the dishes one should only be washing the dishes, which means that while washing the dishes one should be completely aware of the fact that one is washing the dishes. At first glance, that might seem a little silly: why put so much stress on a simple thing? But that's precisely the point. The fact that I am standing there and washing the dishes is a wondrous reality. I'm being completely myself, following my breath, conscious of my presence, and conscious of my thoughts and actions.

THICH NAT HAHN

A little simplification would be the first
step toward rational living, I think.
FLEANOR ROOSEVELT

• • • • •

If you want to feel rich, just count all the
things you have that money can't buy.
UNKNOWN

• • • • •

He who buys what he does
not need steals from himself.
UNKNOWN

I have come to terms with the future.
From this day onward I will walk easy
on the earth. Plant trees. . . .
Live in harmony with all creatures.
I will restore the earth where I am.
Use no more of its resources than I need.
And listen, listen to what it is telling me.
M. J. SLIM HOOEY

An elegant sufficiency, content, retirement, rural quiet,
friendship, books, ease and alternate labor,
useful life, progressive virtue, and approving heaven!

JAMES THOMSON

• • • • • • •

Good heavens, of what uncostly material is our
earthly happiness composed. . .if we only knew it.
What incomes have we not had from a flower,
and how unfailing are the dividends of the seasons.

JAMES RUSSELL LOWELL

A man must be able to cut a knot,
for everything cannot be untied;
he must know how to disengage what
is essential from the detail in which it
is enwrapped, for everything cannot
be equally considered; in a word,
he must be able to simplify his duties,
his business, and his life.

HENRI FREDERIC AMIEL

Dare to be naive.
BUCKMINSTER FULLER

• • • • • • •

If your mind isn't clouded by unnecessary things,
this is the best season of your life.
WU-MEN

So, friends, every day do something that won't compute. Love the Lord. Love the world. Work for nothing. Take all that you have and be poor. Love someone who does not deserve it.

WENDELL BERRY

But he's already made it plain how to live, what to do, what God is looking for in men and women. It's quite simple: Do what is fair and just to your neighbor, be compassionate and loyal in your love, and don't take yourself too seriously—take God seriously.

MICAH 6:8 MSG

Man is an over-complicated organism.
If he is doomed to extinction he will
die out for want of simplicity.
Ezra Pound

• • • • • • • •

Poor and content is rich and rich enough.
William Shakespeare

Practically speaking, a life that is vowed to
simplicity, appropriate boldness, good humor,
gratitude, unstinting work and play, and lots of
walking brings us close to the actual existing
world and its wholeness.

GARY SNYDER

· · · · ·

A garden isn't meant to be useful. It's for joy.

RUMER GODDEN

· · · · ·

Happiness depends, as Nature shows,
less on exterior things than most suppose.

WILLIAM COWPER

We should all do what, in the long run,
gives us joy, even if it is only picking
grapes or sorting the laundry.
E. B. WHITE

• • • • •

In the hope of reaching the moon, men fail
to see the flowers that blossom at their feet.
ALBERT SCHWEITZER

Simplicity, clarity, singleness:
these are the attributes that give our
lives power and vividness and joy.
RICHARD HALLOWAY

• • • • •

Our guiding idea has been,
other things being equal,
complexity in a model indicates
vacuousness rather than sophistication.
J. M. MACIEJOWSKI

Simple pleasures are the
last refuge of the complex.
OSCAR WILDE

• • • • •

The day is of infinite length for him who
knows how to appreciate and use it.
GOETHE

• • • • •

Plurality should not be
assumed without necessity.
WILLIAM OF OCKHAM

You can never get enough of what you
don't need to make you happy.
ERIC HOFFER

· · · · ·

I'd like to live as a poor man
with lots of money.
PABLO PICASSO

· · · · ·

Two wings lift a person up from
earthly concerns: simplicity in intention,
and purity in feeling.
THOMAS À KEMPIS

The world has to learn that the actual pleasure derived from material things is of rather low quality on the whole and less even in quantity than it looks to those who have not tried it.

Oliver Wendell Holmes

· · · · ·

The noble simplicity in the works of nature only too often originates in the noble shortsightedness of him who observes it.

G. C. Lichtenberg

What would be the best gift we could give our children? I think it would be the strength to live simpler lives: the ability to find the greatest joy in God's small quiet gifts rather than in prestige and money. What good does all our busyness do, if our children do not know how to appreciate a sunset or truly taste a sun-warmed strawberry? But this is a gift we must first unwrap ourselves. We cannot hope to give it to our children in an e-mail we send them between appointments at the office.

SADIE MILLHOUSE

God's Message: "Heaven's my throne, earth is my footstool. What sort of house could you build for me? What holiday spot reserve for me? I made all this! I own all this!" God's Decree. "But there is something I'm looking for: a person simple and plain, reverently responsive to what I say."

ISAIAH 66:1–2 MSG

Yes, in the poor man's garden grow far more than
herbs and flowers—kind thoughts, contentment,
peace of mind, and joy for weary hours.
UNKNOWN

• • • • • •

Life is beautiful in its simplicity.
THOMAS MATTHIESSEN

• • • • • •

Simplicity of character is no hindrance
to the subtlety of intellect.
JOHN MORLEY

But there is a spirituality that is more like a lowly emanation from the most humble and earthbound things; that of a particular house, a garden, a neighborhood, a grove of trees, a pristine beach, a holy well, a field of wheat. Here spirituality is indistinguishable from enchantment, for in an enchanted world the things of nature and even of culture reek of holiness. Enchantment is nothing more than spirituality deeply rooted in the earth.

THOMAS MOORE

The ordinary arts we practice every day
at home are of more importance to the soul
than their simplicity might suggest.
THOMAS MOORE

• • • • •

You can't have everything;
where would you put it?
STEVEN WRIGHT

• • • • •

The whole is simpler than
the sum of its parts.
WILLARD GIBBS

Simplicity involves unburdening your life, and living more lightly with fewer distractions that interfere with a high-quality life, as defined uniquely by each individual. You will find people living simply in large cities, rural areas, and everything in between.

LINDA BREEN PIERCE

For peace of mind, we need to resign
as general manager of the universe.
LARRY EISENBERG

•   •   •   •   •

My themes will not be far-fetched.
I will tell of homely everyday
phenomena and adventures.
HENRY DAVID THOREAU

•   •   •   •   •

To simplify complications is
the first essential of success.
GEORGE EARLE BUCKLE

Everything is complex and everything is simple.
The rose has no *why* attached to it.
It blooms because it blooms, with no thought of
itself or desire to be seen. What could be more
complicated than a rose for someone who wants
to understand it? What could be simpler for
someone who wants nothing?
The complexity of thinking, the simplicity of beholding.
ANDRE COMTE-SPONVILLE

He lacks much who has no aptitude for idleness.
LOUISE BEEBE WILDER

• • • • • • • • •

One must first seek to love plants and nature,
and then to cultivate that happy peace of mind
which is satisfied with little. He will be happier
if he has no rigid and arbitrary ideals,
for gardens are coquettish,
particularly with the novice.
LIBERTY HYDE BAILEY

I believe we would be happier to have a personal revolution in our individual lives and go back to simpler living and more direct thinking. It is the simple things of life that make living worthwhile, the sweet fundamental things such as love and duty, work and rest, and living close to nature. There are not hothouse blossoms that can compare in beauty and fragrance with my bouquet of wildflowers.

LAURA INGALLS WILDER

The LORD protects those of childlike faith;
I was facing death, and he saved me.
PSALM 116:6 NLT

• • • • •

The answer's simple: Live right, speak the
truth, despise exploitation, refuse bribes,
reject violence, avoid evil amusements.
This is how you raise your standard of living!
A safe and stable way to live. A nourishing,
satisfying way to live.
ISAIAH 33:15–16 MSG

We shall never know all the
good that a simple smile can do.
MOTHER TERESA

It is always the simple things that change our lives. And these things never happen when you are looking for them to happen. Life will reveal answers at the pace life wishes to do so. You feel like running, but life is on a stroll.

DONALD MILLER

• • • • •

We cannot change our past. We cannot change the fact that people act in a certain way. We cannot change the inevitable. The only thing we can do is play on the one string we have, and that is our attitude.

CHARLES R. SWINDOLL

Success comes from taking the initiative
and following up. . .persisting. . .
eloquently expressing the depth of your love.
What simple action could you take today
to produce a new momentum toward
success in your life?
TONY ROBBINS

• • • • • • • •

If you want to be successful, it's just this simple.
Know what you are doing. Love what you are doing.
And believe in what you are doing.
WILL ROGERS

I believe that a simple and unassuming manner of life is best for everyone, best both for the body and the mind.

ALBERT EINSTEIN

• • • • • •

The firm, the enduring, the simple, and the modest are near to virtue.

CONFUCIUS

When the solution is simple, God is answering.
ALBERT EINSTEIN

• • • • •

Success is nothing more than a few simple
disciplines, practiced every day.
JIM ROHN

• • • • •

Our pleasures were simple—
they included survival.
DWIGHT D. EISENHOWER

In dwelling, live close to the ground. In thinking, keep to the simple. In conflict, be fair and generous. In governing, don't try to control. In work, do what you enjoy. In family life, be completely present.

LAO TZU

• • • • •

Human subtlety will never devise an invention more beautiful, more simple, or more direct than does nature, because in her inventions nothing is lacking and nothing is superfluous.

LEONARDO DA VINCI

A return to first principles in a republic is sometimes caused by the simple virtues of one man. His good example has such an influence that the good men strive to imitate him, and the wicked are ashamed to lead a life so contrary to his example.

NICCOLO MACHIAVELLI

I have a simple philosophy: Fill what's empty.
Empty what's full. Scratch where it itches.
ALICE ROOSEVELT LONGWORTH

• • • • •

But what is happiness except the simple
harmony between a man and the life he leads?
ALBERT CAMUS

A man's work is nothing but this
slow trek to rediscover, through the
detours of art, those two or three
great and simple images in whose
presence his heart first opened.
ALBERT CAMUS

*These children are at the very center of
life in the kingdom. Mark this: Unless you
accept God's kingdom in the simplicity
of a child, you'll never get in.*
MARK 10:14–15 MSG

• • • • • •

*"And when you come before God,
don't turn that into a theatrical production either.
All these people making a regular show out
of their prayers, hoping for stardom!
Do you think God sits in a box seat?"*
MATTHEW 6:5 MSG

There is no power on earth that can neutralize the influence of a high, simple, and useful life.
BOOKER T. WASHINGTON

• • • • •

There is nothing so strong or safe in an emergency of life as the simple truth.
CHARLES DICKENS

The right thing to do. . .
is always simple and direct.
CALVIN COOLIDGE

• • • • •

They criticize me for harping on the obvious;
if all the folks in the United States would do
the few simple things they know they ought
to do, most of our big problems would
take care of themselves.
CALVIN COOLIDGE

Everything deep is also simple and can be reproduced simply as long as its reference to the whole truth is maintained. But what matters is not what is witty but what is true.

ALBERT SCHWEITZER

• • • • •

More helpful than all wisdom is one draught of simple human pity that will not forsake us.

GEORGE ELIOT

Simplicity is indeed often the sign
of truth and a criterion of beauty.
MAHLON HOAGLAND

• • • • •

Simplicity is the nature of great souls.
PAPA RAMADAS

• • • • •

A vocabulary of truth and simplicity
will be of service throughout your life.
WINSTON CHURCHILL

Enjoy the simple, the natural, and the plain.
Along with that comes the ability to do things
spontaneously and have them work.
BENJAMIN HOFF

• • • • •

Fishing is much more than fish.
It is the great occasion when we may
return to the fine simplicity of our forefathers.
HERBERT HOOVER

Never again will I make the simple into the complex. Something of true value does not become more valuable because it becomes complicated. Experience and conditions come and go; complications arise and fall away, but the simple action of God is eternal in the universe.

DONALD CURTIS

Grandeur and beauty are so very opposite, that you often diminish the one as you increase the other. Variety is most akin to the latter, simplicity to the former.

WILLIAM SHENSTONE

•   •   •   •   •

I would not give a fig for the simplicity this side of complexity, but I would give my life for the simplicity on the other side of complexity.

OLIVER WENDELL HOLMES

I take a simple view of living.
It is, keep your eyes open and get on with it.
SIR LAURENCE OLIVIER

• • • • • •

It is simplicity that makes the uneducated
more effective than the educated when
addressing popular audiences.
ARISTOTLE

Don't evaluate your life in terms of achievements, trivial or monumental, along the way. . . instead, wake up and appreciate everything you encounter along the path. Enjoy the flowers that are there for your pleasure. Tune in to the sunrise, the little children, the laughter, the rain, and the birds. Drink it all in. . .there is no way to happiness; happiness is the way.

DR. WAYNE W. DYER

Sometimes I would almost have people take away years of my life than take away a moment.

PEARL BAILEY

• • • • • •

Anyone can carry his burden, however hard, until nightfall. Anyone can do his work, however hard, for one day. Anyone can live sweetly, patiently, lovingly, purely, till the sun goes down. And this is all that life really means.

ROBERT LOUIS STEVENSON

How far you go in life depends on your being tender with the young, compassionate with the aged, sympathetic with the striving, and tolerant of the weak and the strong; because someday in life you will have been all of these.

GEORGE WASHINGTON CARVER

To see a world in a grain of sand
And a heaven in a wild flower,
Hold infinity in the palm of your hand
And eternity in an hour.

WILLIAM BLAKE

To fill the hour—that is happiness;
to fill the hour, and leave no crevice
for a repentance or an approval.
RALPH WALDO EMERSON

• • • • •

Between the house and the store there are
little pockets of happiness: a bird, a garden,
a friend's greeting, a child's smile, a cat in the
sunshine needing a stroke. Recognize them or
ignore them. It's always up to you.
PAM BROWN

That the birds of worry and care fly above your
head, this you cannot change. But that they
build nests in your hair, this you can prevent.

CHINESE PROVERB

• • • • •

He who smiles rather than rages
is always the stronger.

JAPANESE PROVERB

• • • • •

The greatest revelation is stillness.

LAO TZU

Contentment. . .comes as the infallible
result of great acceptances,
great humilities—of not trying to make
ourselves this or that
(to conform to some dramatized version
of ourselves), but of surrendering
ourselves to the fullness of life—
of letting life flow through us.
DAVID GRAYSON

The serene have not opted out of life.
They see more widely, love more dearly,
rejoice in the things the frantic mind
no longer sees or hears.
PAM BROWN

• • • • •

Leave home in the sunshine:
dance through a meadow—or sit by a stream
and just be. The lilt of the water will gather your
worries and carry them down to the sea.
J. DONALD WALTERS

Work is not always required of a man.
There is such a thing as sacred idleness,
the cultivation of which is now fearfully neglected.
GEORGE MACDONALD

• • • • • •

If you can spend a perfectly useless
afternoon in a perfectly useless manner,
you have learned how to live.
LIN YUTANG

Teach me the art of creating islands of stillness,
in which I can absorb the beauty of everyday
things: clouds, trees, a snatch of music. . .
MARION STROUD

• • • • • • •

Happiness is as a butterfly, which, when pursued,
is always beyond our grasp, but which,
if you will sit down quietly, may alight upon you.
NATHANIEL HAWTHORNE

Do not let trifles disturb your tranquility of mind. . . . Life is too precious to be sacrificed for the nonessential and transient. . . . Ignore the inconsequential.

GRENVILLE KLEISER

• • • • • •

Life just is. You have to flow with it. Give yourself to the moment. Let it happen.

JERRY BROWN

The Indians prefer the soft sound of the wind darting over the face of the pond, the smell of the wind itself cleansed by the midday rain, or scented with pinion pine.

CHIEF SEATTLE

There is, perhaps, no solitary sensation so exquisite as that of slumbering on the grass or hay, shaded from the hot sun by a tree, with the consciousness of a fresh, light air running through the wide atmosphere, and the sky stretching far overhead upon all sides.

LEIGH HUNT

Arranging a bowl of flowers in the morning can
give a sense of quiet in a crowded day—
like writing a poem, or saying a prayer.
ANNE MORROW LINDBERGH

• • • • •

Here will we sit and let the sounds of music
creep in our ears: soft stillness and the night
become the touches of sweet harmony.
WILLIAM SHAKESPEARE

If we are not happy, if we are not
peaceful, we cannot share peace and
happiness with others, even those we love,
those who live under the same roof.
If we are peaceful, if we are happy,
we can smile and blossom like a flower,
and everyone in our family, our entire
society, will benefit from our peace.
THICH NHAT HANH

If only I may grow:
firmer, simpler, quieter, warmer.
DAG HAMMARSKJOLD

• • • • •

I expand and live in the warm
day like corn and melons.
RALPH WALDO EMERSON

• • • • •

The poor long for riches and the rich for heaven,
but the wise long for a state of tranquility.
RAMA

And so, while others miserably pledge themselves to the insatiable pursuit of ambition and brief power,
I will be stretched out in the shade, singing.

FRAY LUIS DE LEON

• • • • •

I have lived through much and now I think I have found what is needed for happiness. A quiet, secluded life in the country with the possibility of being useful to people.

LEO TOLSTOY

We all grow up at last and lose that first sharp
vision of the world. We miss dew sparkle,
leaf shadow, spider scuttle, puddle shine.
We waste time on worry. And we find the days
sweep by, each blurred, each like the other.

PAM BROWN

· · · · ·

Life is a succession of moments.
To live each one is to succeed.

CORITA KENT

People, for the sake of getting
a living, forget to live.
MARGARET FULLER

• • • • •

Write it on your heart that every
day is the best day in the year.
RALPH WALDO EMERSON

Let us spend one day as deliberately
as nature, and not be thrown off the
track by every nutshell and mosquito's
wing that falls on the rails. Let us rise
early and fast, or break fast, gently and
without perturbation; let company come
and let company go, let the bells ring
and the children cry.
HENRY DAVID THOREAU

Make voyages. Attempt them. That's all there is.
ELAINE DUNDY

• • • • • • • •

Do not linger to gather flowers to keep them,
but walk on, for flowers will keep
blooming all your way.
RABINDRANATH TAGORE

We must be willing to let go of the life we have
planned so as to have the life that is waiting for us.
E. M. FORSTER

• • • • • • •

Forget not that the earth delights to feel your bare
feet and the winds long to play with your hair.
KAHLIL GIBRAN

Laughter is immeasurable. Be joyful though
you have considered all the facts.
WENDELL BERRY

•   •   •   •   •

From what we get, we can make a living;
what we give, however, makes a life.
ARTHUR ASHE

To be content with little is hard,
to be content with much, impossible.
BARONNESS MARIE VON
EBNER-ESCHENBACH

Life is not a problem to be solved
but a reality to be experienced.
S<small>OREN</small> K<small>IERKEGAARD</small>

• • • • • • • •

The real things haven't changed. It is still best to
be honest and truthful; to make the most of what
we have; to be happy with simple pleasures;
and have courage when things go wrong.
L<small>AURA</small> I<small>NGALLS</small> W<small>ILDER</small>

For most of life, nothing wonderful happens. If you don't enjoy getting up and working and finishing your work and sitting down to a meal with family or friends, then the chances are you're not going to be very happy. If someone bases his happiness or unhappiness on major events like a great new job, huge amounts of money, a flawlessly happy marriage, or a trip to Paris, that person isn't going to be happy much of the time. If, on the other hand, happiness depends on a good breakfast, flowers in the yard, a drink, or a nap, then we are more likely to live with quite a bit of happiness.

ANDY ROONEY

To be without some of the things you want
is an indispensable part of happiness.
BERTRAND RUSSELL

• • • • •

To become a happy person, have a clean soul,
eyes that see romance in the commonplace,
a child's heart, and spiritual simplicity.
NORMAN VINCENT PEALE

How simple and frugal a thing is happiness:
a glass of wine, a roast chestnut, a wretched
little brazier, the sound of the sea. . . .
All that is required to feel that here and now
is happiness is a simple, frugal heart.
NIKOS KAZANTZAKIS

• • • • •

Be content with such things as ye have.
HEBREWS 13:5 KJV

Whenever you are sincerely pleased,
you are nourished.
RALPH WALDO EMERSON

• • • • • • • •

He is richest who is content with least;
for content is the wealth of nature.
SOCRATES

Happiness doesn't depend upon who
you are or what you have;
it depends solely upon what you think.
DALE CARNEGIE

• • • • • • • •

Seek out the good and your
mind will fill with happiness.
JOHN MARKS TEMPLETON

• • • • • • • •

It is the mind that maketh good of ill,
that maketh wretch or happy,
rich or poor.
EDMUND SPENSER

It's good to be just plain happy; it's a little better
to know that you're happy; but to understand that
you're happy and to know why and how. . .
and still be happy, be happy in the being and the
knowing, well that is beyond happiness, that is bliss.

HENRY MILLER

If you can walk, you can dance.
If you can talk, you can sing.
ZIMBABWE PROVERB

This is the true joy in life, the being used for a purpose recognized by yourself as a mighty one; the being thoroughly worn out before you are thrown on the scrap heap; the being a force of nature instead of a feverish little clod of ailments and grievances complaining that the world will not devote itself to making you happy.

GEORGE BERNARD SHAW

One must marry one's feelings to one's beliefs
and ideas. That is probably the only way to
achieve a measure of harmony in one's life.

ETTY HILLESUM

• • • • • • •

Give me beauty in the inward soul;
may the outward and the inward man be at one.

SOCRATES

The heart of the wise man lies
quiet like limpid water.
CAMEROONIAN SAYING

• • • • • • •

Be calm. Dismiss the busy thoughts
that trouble your mind. Let them go.
Rest in the simple fact: God loves you.
ROBIN PATTERSON

And all the windows
of my heart
I open to the day.

JOHN GREENLEAF WHITTIER

In character, in manner, in style,
in all things, the supreme
excellence is simplicity.
HENRY WADSWORTH LONGFELLOW

There is no season such delight can bring
as summer, autumn, winter and the spring.
WILLIAM BROWNE

• • • • • • •

Stop and touch the earth, and receive its influence;
touch the flower, and feel its life; face the wind,
and have its meaning; let the sunlight fall on the
open hand as if you could hold it. Something may
be grasped from them all, invisible yet strong.
It is the sense of a wider existence—
wider and higher.
RICHARD JEFFERIES

However limited your life is,
meet it and live it: do not shun
it and call it hard names.
Cultivate poverty like a garden herb, like sage.
Do not trouble yourself much to get
new things. . . . Sell your clothes
and keep your thoughts.
HENRY DAVID THOREAU